50 German Pastry Recipes for Home

By: Kelly Johnson

Table of Contents

- Apfelstrudel (Apple Strudel)
- Schwarzwalder Kirschtorte (Black Forest Cake)
- Berliner Pfannkuchen (Berliners)
- Streuselkuchen (Crumb Cake)
- Lebkuchen (Gingerbread)
- Buttergebäck (Butter Cookies)
- Marzipan treats
- Stollen (Christmas Fruit Bread)
- Quarkkuchen (Quark Cheesecake)
- Mohnkuchen (Poppy Seed Cake)
- Zimtschnecken (Cinnamon Rolls)
- Windbeutel (Cream Puffs)
- Krapfen (Filled Doughnuts)
- Bienenstich (Bee Sting Cake)
- Nussecken (Nut Corners)
- Pfeffernüsse (Spice Cookies)
- Schneeballen (Snowball Cookies)
- Streusel (Crumbles)
- Puddingteilchen (Pudding Pastries)
- Strudel (Filled Pastry)
- Honigkuchen (Honey Cake)
- Käsekuchen (Cheesecake)
- Mandelhörnchen (Almond Crescents)
- Eclairs (Cream-Filled Pastries)
- Baumkuchen (Tree Cake)
- Kuchen (Cakes)
- Plätzchen (Cookies)
- Kirschkuchen (Cherry Cake)
- Rhabarberkuchen (Rhubarb Cake)
- Mürbeteig (Shortcrust Pastry)
- Hefezopf (Yeast Braid)
- Franzbrötchen (Cinnamon Pastries)
- Aprikosenkuchen (Apricot Cake)
- Eierschecke (Layered Cake)
- Schokoladentorte (Chocolate Cake)

- Erdbeerkuchen (Strawberry Cake)
- Butterkuchen (Butter Cake)
- Vanillekipferl (Vanilla Crescents)
- Kokosmakronen (Coconut Macaroons)
- Früchtebrot (Fruit Bread)
- Buchteln (Sweet Rolls)
- Dampfnudeln (Steamed Dumplings)
- Kirschplotzer (Cherry Tart)
- Mohntorte (Poppy Seed Tart)
- Linzer Torte (Linzer Tart)
- Schmandkuchen (Sour Cream Cake)
- Zwetschgenkuchen (Plum Cake)
- Birnenkuchen (Pear Cake)
- Zwetschgenknödel (Plum Dumplings)
- Käse-Sahne-Torte (Cheese Cream Cake)

Apfelstrudel (Apple Strudel)

Ingredients:

For the pastry dough:

- 2 cups all-purpose flour
- 1/4 teaspoon salt
- 2 tablespoons vegetable oil
- 3/4 cup warm water
- 1 tablespoon white vinegar

For the filling:

- 4 large apples (such as Granny Smith or Braeburn), peeled, cored, and thinly sliced
- 1/2 cup granulated sugar
- 1/2 cup breadcrumbs
- 1/2 cup raisins (optional)
- 1 teaspoon ground cinnamon
- 1/4 teaspoon ground nutmeg
- 1/4 cup melted butter
- Powdered sugar, for dusting

Instructions:

1. Preheat your oven to 375°F (190°C). Line a baking sheet with parchment paper.
2. In a large mixing bowl, combine the flour and salt. Make a well in the center and add the vegetable oil, warm water, and white vinegar. Mix until a dough forms. Knead the dough on a floured surface until it becomes smooth and elastic. Form the dough into a ball, cover it with a clean kitchen towel, and let it rest for 30 minutes.
3. Meanwhile, prepare the filling. In a separate bowl, toss the sliced apples with granulated sugar, breadcrumbs, raisins (if using), cinnamon, and nutmeg until evenly coated.
4. Roll out the dough on a lightly floured surface into a thin rectangle, about 1/8 inch thick. Brush the melted butter over the entire surface of the dough.

5. Spread the prepared apple filling evenly over the dough, leaving about 1 inch of space around the edges. Fold the shorter edges of the dough over the filling, then carefully roll the dough into a log, sealing the edges.
6. Transfer the strudel onto the prepared baking sheet, seam side down. Brush the top of the strudel with additonal melted butter.
7. Bake the strudel in the preheated oven for 30-35 minutes, or until the pastry is golden brown and crisp.
8. Remove the strudel from the oven and let it cool slightly before slicing. Dust with powdered sugar before serving.
9. Enjoy your homemade Apfe strudel warm or at room temperature, with a dollop of whipped cream or a scoop of vanilla ice cream, if desired. Guten Appetit!

Schwarzwalder Kirschtorte (Black Forest Cake)

Ingredients:

For the chocolate cake layers:

- 1 and 3/4 cups all-purpose flour
- 3/4 cup unsweetened cocoa powder
- 2 cups granulated sugar
- 2 teaspoons baking powder
- 1 teaspoon baking soda
- 1 teaspoon salt
- 2 large eggs
- 1 cup milk
- 1/2 cup vegetable oil
- 2 teaspoons vanilla extract
- 1 cup boiling water

For the cherry filling:

- 3 cups pitted cherries (fresh or canned)
- 1/4 cup granulated sugar
- 1 tablespoon cornstarch
- 2 tablespoons Kirsch (cherry brandy), optional

For the whipped cream:

- 2 cups heavy cream, chilled
- 1/4 cup powdered sugar
- 1 teaspoon vanilla extract

For decoration:

- Chocolate shavings or curls
- Maraschino cherries (optional)

Instructions:

1. Preheat your oven to 350°F (175°C). Grease and flour two 9-inch round cake pans.

2. In a large mixing bowl, sift together the flour, cocoa powder, sugar, baking powder, baking soda, and salt.
3. Add the eggs, milk, oil, and vanilla extract to the dry ingredients. Beat on medium speed for 2 minutes. Stir in the boiling water until the batter is well combined (it will be thin).
4. Pour the batter evenly into the prepared cake pans. Bake in the preheated oven for 30 to 35 minutes, or until a toothpick inserted into the center of the cakes comes out clean.
5. Allow the cakes to cool in the pans for 10 minutes, then transfer them to a wire rack to cool completely.
6. While the cakes are cooling, prepare the cherry filling. In a saucepan, combine the pitted cherries, sugar, and cornstarch. Cook over medium heat, stirring constantly, until the mixture thickens. Remove from heat and stir in the Kirsch, if using. Let the cherry filling cool completely.
7. To make the whipped cream, beat the chilled heavy cream, powdered sugar, and vanilla extract together until stiff peaks form.
8. Once the cakes have cooled completely, use a serrated knife to level the tops if necessary. Place one cake layer on a serving plate. Spread a layer of whipped cream over the cake, followed by a layer of cherry filling. Top with the second cake layer.
9. Frost the top and sides of the cake with the remaining whipped cream. Decorate with chocolate shavings or curls and maraschino cherries, if desired.
10. Chill the cake in the refrigerator for at least 1 hour before serving to allow the flavors to meld together. Enjoy your homemade Schwarzwälder Kirschtorte!

Berliner Pfannkuchen (Berliners)

Ingredients:

For the dough:

- 3 and 1/2 cups all-purpose flour
- 1/4 cup granulated sugar
- 1 teaspoon salt
- 2 and 1/4 teaspoons active dry yeast
- 3/4 cup milk, warmed to about 110°F (43°C)
- 3 large eggs
- 1/4 cup unsalted butter, softened
- Vegetable oil, for frying

For the filling:

- Your choice of jam, jelly, or pastry cream

For the topping:

- Powdered sugar, for dusting

Instructions:

1. In a large mixing bowl, combine 2 cups of flour, sugar, salt, and yeast. Stir well to combine.
2. In a separate bowl, whisk together the warm milk and eggs. Pour the milk mixture into the dry ingredients and mix until a sticky dough forms.
3. Add the softened butter to the dough and continue to mix until the butter is fully incorporated.
4. Gradually add the remaining 1 and 1/2 cups of flour, kneading the dough until it becomes smooth and elastic. You may need to add a little more flour if the dough is too sticky.
5. Place the dough in a lightly greased bowl, cover it with a clean kitchen towel, and let it rise in a warm place for about 1 hour, or until doubled in size.

6. Once the dough has risen, punch it down and turn it out onto a floured surface. Roll out the dough to about 1/4 inch thickness.
7. Using a round cutter or drinking glass, cut out circles of dough. Place a small spoonful of your desired filling in the center of each circle.
8. Fold the dough over the filling and pinch the edges to seal, forming a ball. Place the filled doughnuts on a lightly floured surface and let them rest for about 15-20 minutes.
9. In a large, deep skillet or Dutch oven, heat vegetable oil to 350°F (175°C). Carefully add the filled doughnuts to the hot oil, frying in batches until they are golden brown on all sides, about 2-3 minutes per side.
10. Remove the Berliners from the oil using a slotted spoon and drain them on paper towels to remove excess oil.
11. Once the Berliners have cooled slightly, dust them generously with powdered sugar.
12. Serve the Berliners warm or at room temperature. Enjoy these delightful German pastries as a sweet treat any time of day!

Streuselkuchen (Crumb Cake)

Ingredients:

For the cake base:

- 2 cups all-purpose flour
- 1/2 cup granulated sugar
- 1 teaspoon baking powder
- 1/4 teaspoon salt
- 1/2 cup unsalted butter, cold and cubed
- 1 large egg
- 1/2 cup milk
- 1 teaspoon vanilla extract

For the streusel topping:

- 1 and 1/2 cups all-purpose flour
- 3/4 cup granulated sugar
- 1/2 cup unsalted butter, melted
- 1 teaspoon ground cinnamon (optional)

Instructions:

1. Preheat your oven to 350°F (175°C). Grease and flour a 9x13-inch baking pan.
2. In a large mixing bowl, combine the flour, sugar, baking powder, and salt for the cake base. Cut in the cold cubed butter using a pastry cutter or fork until the mixture resembles coarse crumbs.
3. In a separate bowl, whisk together the egg, milk, and vanilla extract. Pour the wet ingredients into the dry ingredients and mix until just combined. The batter will be thick.
4. Spread the batter evenly into the prepared baking pan, using a spatula to smooth the top.
5. In another bowl, combine the flour, sugar, melted butter, and ground cinnamon (if using) for the streusel topping. Mix until crumbly.
6. Sprinkle the streusel topping evenly over the cake batter in the pan.

7. Bake in the preheated oven for 25-30 minutes, or until the streusel is golden brown and a toothpick inserted into the center of the cake comes out clean.
8. Remove the streuselkuchen from the oven and allow it to cool in the pan for about 10-15 minutes.
9. Once cooled slightly, cut the streuselkuchen into squares and serve warm or at room temperature.
10. Enjoy your homemade Streuselkuchen with a cup of coffee or tea for a delightful snack or dessert!

Lebkuchen (Gingerbread)

Ingredients:

For the Lebkuchen dough:

- 3 cups all-purpose flour
- 1 teaspoon baking powder
- 1/2 teaspoon baking soda
- 1 tablespoon ground cinnamon
- 1 teaspoon ground cloves
- 1 teaspoon ground nutmeg
- 1/2 teaspoon ground ginger
- 1/4 teaspoon ground allspice
- 1/4 teaspoon salt
- 1/2 cup unsalted butter, softened
- 1/2 cup granulated sugar
- 1/2 cup packed brown sugar
- 2 large eggs
- 1/2 cup honey
- 1/4 cup molasses
- 1/4 cup milk

For the glaze:

- 1 cup powdered sugar
- 2-3 tablespoons milk
- 1/2 teaspoon vanilla extract

Instructions:

1. Preheat your oven to 350°F (175°C). Line baking sheets with parchment paper.
2. In a medium bowl, whisk together the flour, baking powder, baking soda, cinnamon, cloves, nutmeg, ginger, allspice, and salt. Set aside.
3. In a large mixing bowl, cream together the softened butter, granulated sugar, and brown sugar until light and fluffy.

4. Add the eggs one at a time, beating well after each addition. Then mix in the honey, molasses, and milk until well combined.
5. Gradual y add the dry ingredients to the wet ingredients, mixing until a soft dough forms. The dough will be slightly sticky.
6. Drop rounded tablespoons of dough onto the prepared baking sheets, spacing them about 2 inches apart.
7. Bake in the preheated oven for 10-12 minutes, or until the edges are set and the tops are slightly firm to the touch.
8. Remove the Lebkuchen from the oven and let them cool on the baking sheets for 5 minutes before transferring them to a wire rack to cool completely.
9. While the Lebkuchen are cooling, prepare the glaze by whisking together the powdered sugar, milk, and vanilla extract until smooth. Add more milk if needed to reach your desired consistency.
10. Once the Lebkuchen have cooled completely, drizzle the glaze over the tops using a spoon or piping bag.
11. Let the glaze set before serving or storing the Lebkuchen in an airtight container at room temperature.
12. Enjoy your homemade Lebkuchen as a festive holiday treat or anytime you're craving a deliciously spiced gingerbread cookie!

Buttergebäck (Butter Cookies)

Ingredients:

- 1 cup unsalted butter, softened
- 1/2 cup granulated sugar
- 2 cups all-purpose flour
- 1/4 teaspoon salt
- 1 teaspoon vanilla extract
- Optional: Additional granulated sugar for coating (for sugar cookies)

Instructions:

1. Preheat your oven to 350°F (175°C). Line baking sheets with parchment paper.
2. In a large mixing bowl, cream together the softened butter and granulated sugar until light and fluffy.
3. Add the vanilla extract and mix until well combined.
4. In a separate bowl, whisk together the flour and salt.
5. Gradually add the dry ingredients to the butter mixture, mixing until a soft dough forms. Be careful not to overmix.
6. If you'd like to make sugar-coated butter cookies, shape the dough into small balls (about 1 inch in diameter). Roll each ball in granulated sugar until coated, then place them on the prepared baking sheets. If you prefer plain butter cookies, simply shape the dough into small balls and place them on the baking sheets.
7. Using a fork or cookie stamp, gently flatten each ball of dough to your desired thickness.
8. Bake the cookies in the preheated oven for 10-12 minutes, or until the edges are lightly golden.
9. Remove the cookies from the oven and let them cool on the baking sheets for a few minutes before transferring them to a wire rack to cool completely.
10. Once cooled, store the Buttergebäck in an airtight container at room temperature.
11. Enjoy these deliciously buttery cookies with a cup of tea or coffee, or share them with friends and family during gatherings or holidays. They also make wonderful gifts when packaged in a decorative tin or box!

Marzipan treats

Marzipan treats are a delightful confectionery made from ground almonds and sugar, often flavored with almond extract and shaped into various forms. Here are two classic marzipan treats:

Marzipan Balls:
1. Ingredients:
- 200g (7 oz) marzipan

1/2 cup powdered sugar (for coating)
- Instructions:
1. Pinch off small portions of marzipan and roll them into balls between your palms.
2. Roll each ball in powdered sugar until fully coated.
3. Place the coated marzipan balls on a baking sheet lined with parchment paper.
4. Let them air dry for a few hours until the coating has set.
5. Store the marzipan balls in an airtight container at room temperature.

Marzipan Fruits:
6. Ingredients:
- Marzipan

Food coloring (optional)
- Instructions:
1. Divide the marzipan into small portions.
2. Shape each portion into fruit shapes such as apples, pears, oranges, or strawberries.
3. Use food coloring to paint the marzipan fruits to resemble their natural colors. For example, paint red on apples, green on pears, orange on oranges, etc.
4. Use a toothpick to add details like seeds on apples or dimples on oranges.
5. Let the painted marzipan fruits air dry on a baking sheet lined with parchment paper.
6. Once dry, store the marzipan fruits in an airtight container at room temperature.

These marzipan treats are perfect for snacking, gifting, or decorating cakes and desserts. Enjoy the rich almond flavor and smooth texture of homemade marzipan confections!

Stollen (Christmas Fruit Bread)

Ingredients:

For the dough:

- 4 cups all-purpose flour
- 1/2 cup granulated sugar
- 1 tablespoon active dry yeast
- 1 teaspoon salt
- 1/2 cup unsalted butter, softened
- 3/4 cup warm milk
- 2 large eggs
- 1 teaspoon vanilla extract
- Zest of 1 lemon
- Zest of 1 orange

For the fruit filling:

- 1 cup mixed dried fruits (such as raisins, currants, candied citrus peel)
- 1/4 cup rum or orange juice

For the coating:

- 1/2 cup unsalted butter, melted
- 1/2 cup powdered sugar, for dusting

Instructions:

1. In a small bowl, combine the mixed dried fruits with rum or orange juice. Let them soak for at least 30 minutes, or until plump.
2. In a large mixing bowl, combine 2 cups of flour, granulated sugar, yeast, and salt.
3. Add the softened butter, warm milk, eggs, vanilla extract, lemon zest, and orange zest to the dry ingredients. Mix until a sticky dough forms.
4. Gradually add the remaining 2 cups of flour, kneading the dough until smooth and elastic.

5. Drain the soaked dried fruits and pat them dry with paper towels. Fold the dried fruits into the dough until evenly distributed.
6. Cover the dough with a clean kitchen towel and let it rise in a warm place for about 1 hour, or until doubled in size.
7. Preheat your oven to 350°F (175°C). Line a baking sheet with parchment paper.
8. Punch down the risen dough and transfer it to a lightly floured surface. Shape the dough into an oval loaf, about 10-12 inches long.
9. Place the shaped Stollen on the prepared baking sheet. Cover it loosely with plastic wrap and let it rise for an additional 30 minutes.
10. Bake the Stollen in the preheated oven for 30-35 minutes, or until golden brown and cooked through.
11. Remove the Stollen from the oven and immediately brush it with melted butter while it's still hot.
12. Let the Stollen cool completely on a wire rack. Once cooled, dust it generously with powdered sugar.
13. Slice the Stollen into thick slices and serve. Enjoy this festive Christmas fruit bread with a cup of tea or coffee!
14. Stollen can be stored in an airtight container at room temperature for up to one week. It also freezes well for longer storage.

Quarkkuchen (Quark Cheesecake)

Ingredients:

For the crust:

- 1 and 1/2 cups graham cracker crumbs (or crushed digestive biscuits)
- 1/4 cup granulated sugar
- 1/2 cup unsalted butter, melted

For the filling:

- 2 cups quark (if quark is not available, you can use a mixture of cottage cheese and Greek yogurt)
- 1 cup granulated sugar
- 4 large eggs
- 1/4 cup all-purpose flour
- 1/2 cup heavy cream
- 1 teaspoon vanilla extract
- Zest of 1 lemon

Instructions:

1. Preheat your oven to 350°F (175°C). Grease a 9-inch springform pan and line the bottom with parchment paper.
2. In a mixing bowl, combine the graham cracker crumbs, granulated sugar, and melted butter for the crust. Mix until well combined.
3. Press the crumb mixture evenly into the bottom of the prepared springform pan, using the back of a spoon or your fingers to pack it tightly. Set aside.
4. In a large mixing bowl, beat the quark and granulated sugar together until smooth.
5. Add the eggs, one at a time, beating well after each addition.
6. Gradually add the flour, heavy cream, vanilla extract, and lemon zest, mixing until the filling is smooth and well combined.
7. Pour the filling over the prepared crust in the springform pan, smoothing the top with a spatula.

8. Bake the Quarkkuchen in the preheated oven for 45-50 minutes, or until the edges are set and the center is slightly jiggly.
9. Turn off the oven and leave the Quarkkuchen inside with the oven door slightly ajar for about 30 minutes to cool gradually.
10. Remove the Quarkkuchen from the oven and let it cool completely at room temperature. Then refrigerate for at least 4 hours, or overnight, to chill and set.
11. Once chilled, carefully remove the sides of the springform pan.
12. Slice the Quarkkuchen into wedges and serve chilled. Enjoy the creamy and tangy flavor of this delightful German cheesecake!
13. You can garnish the Quarkkuchen with fresh berries, whipped cream, or a dusting of powdered sugar before serving, if desired.

Mohnkuchen (Poppy Seed Cake)

Ingredients:

For the cake:

- 1 and 1/2 cups all-purpose flour
- 1/2 cup granulated sugar
- 1/2 cup unsalted butter, softened
- 1/2 cup milk
- 2 large eggs
- 1/2 cup ground poppy seeds
- 1/4 cup finely ground almonds (optional)
- 2 teaspoons baking powder
- 1 teaspoon vanilla extract
- Zest of 1 lemon
- Pinch of salt

For the glaze (optional):

- 1/2 cup powdered sugar
- 1-2 tablespoons milk
- 1/2 teaspoon vanilla extract

Instructions:

1. Preheat your oven to 350°F (175°C). Grease and flour a 9-inch round cake pan.
2. In a large mixing bowl, cream together the softened butter and granulated sugar until light and fluffy.
3. Add the eggs, one at a time, beating well after each addition. Stir in the vanilla extract and lemon zest.
4. In a separate bowl, whisk together the flour, ground poppy seeds, ground almonds (if using), baking powder, and salt.
5. Gradually add the dry ingredients to the butter mixture, alternating with the milk, until well combined. Mix until a smooth batter forms.
6. Pour the batter into the prepared cake pan and spread it evenly with a spatula.

7. Bake in the preheated oven for 25-30 minutes, or until a toothpick inserted into the center of the cake comes out clean.
8. Remove the cake from the oven and let it cool in the pan for about 10 minutes before transferring it to a wire rack to cool completely.
9. If desired, prepare the glaze by whisking together the powdered sugar, milk, and vanilla extract until smooth. Drizzle the glaze over the cooled cake.
10. Slice the Mohnkuchen into wedges and serve. Enjoy the deliciously nutty flavor of this classic German poppy seed cake with a cup of coffee or tea!
11. Store any leftover Mohnkuchen in an airtight container at room temperature for up to 3 days.

Zimtschnecken (Cinnamon Rolls)

Ingredients:

For the dough:

- 4 cups all-purpose flour
- 1/3 cup granulated sugar
- 1 teaspoon salt
- 2 and 1/4 teaspoons active dry yeast
- 1 cup milk
- 1/3 cup unsalted butter, softened
- 2 large eggs

For the filling:

- 1/2 cup unsalted butter, softened
- 3/4 cup brown sugar
- 2 tablespoons ground cinnamon

For the icing:

- 1 cup powdered sugar
- 2-3 tablespoons milk
- 1/2 teaspoon vanilla extract

Instructions:

1. In a small saucepan, heat the milk until warm (about 110°F or 45°C), but not hot. Remove from heat and stir in the yeast. Let it sit for about 5 minutes, or until foamy.
2. In a large mixing bowl, combine the flour, granulated sugar, and salt. Add the softened butter and eggs, then pour in the milk-yeast mixture. Stir until a dough forms.
3. Turn the dough out onto a lightly floured surface and knead for about 5-7 minutes, or until smooth and elastic.
4. Place the dough in a greased bowl, cover with a clean kitchen towel, and let it rise in a warm place for about 1 hour, or until doubled in size.
5. While the dough is rising, prepare the filling by mixing together the softened butter, brown sugar, and ground cinnamon until well combined.

6. Once the dough has doubled in size, punch it down and roll it out into a rectangle about 1/4 inch thick.
7. Spread the cinnamon filling evenly over the dough, leaving a small border around the edges.
8. Starting from one long side, tightly roll up the dough into a log. Pinch the seam to seal.
9. Using a sharp knife, slice the dough into about 12 equal-sized rolls.
10. Place the rolls in a greased baking dish, leaving a little space between each roll. Cover with a clean kitchen towel and let them rise for another 30 minutes.
11. Preheat your oven to 350°F (175°C). Bake the cinnamon rolls in the preheated oven for 20-25 minutes, or until golden brown.
12. While the rolls are baking, prepare the icing by whisking together the powdered sugar, milk, and vanilla extract until smooth.
13. Remove the cinnamon rolls from the oven and let them cool slightly before drizzling the icing over the top.
14. Serve the Zimtschnecken warm and enjoy their deliciously sweet and cinnamon-spiced flavor!

Windbeutel (Cream Puffs)

Ingredients:

For the choux pastry:

- 1/2 cup unsalted butter
- 1 cup water
- 1 cup all-purpose flour
- 4 large eggs
- Pinch of salt

For the filling:

- 2 cups heavy cream
- 1/4 cup powdered sugar
- 1 teaspoon vanilla extract

For the topping (optional):

- Powdered sugar, for dusting

Instructions:

1. Preheat your oven to 400°F (200°C). Line a baking sheet with parchment paper.
2. In a medium saucepan, combine the butter, water, and salt. Bring to a boil over medium heat.
3. Reduce the heat to low and add the flour all at once. Stir vigorously with a wooden spoon until the mixture forms a ball and pulls away from the sides of the pan.
4. Transfer the dough to a mixing bowl and let it cool for a few minutes.
5. Add the eggs, one at a time, beating well after each addition, until the dough is smooth and glossy.
6. Spoon the dough into a piping bag fitted with a large round tip (or simply use a spoon). Pipe mounds of dough onto the prepared baking sheet, leaving space between each puff.

7. Bake the cream puffs in the preheated oven for 25-30 minutes, or until puffed and golden brown. Do not open the oven door during baking, as this may cause the cream puffs to collapse.
8. Remove the cream puffs from the oven and let them cool completely on a wire rack.
9. While the cream puffs are cooling, prepare the filling. In a mixing bowl, whip the heavy cream, powdered sugar, and vanilla extract until stiff peaks form.
10. Once the cream puffs are completely cool, use a sharp knife to slice off the tops. Fill each puff with a generous dollop of whipped cream.
11. Replace the tops of the cream puffs and dust them with powdered sugar, if desired.
12. Serve the Windbeutel immediately, or store them in the refrigerator until ready to serve. Enjoy the light and creamy indulgence of homemade Cream Puffs!

Krapfen (Filled Doughnuts)

Ingredients:

For the dough:

- 3 and 1/2 cups all-purpose flour
- 1/2 cup granulated sugar
- 1 packet (2 and 1/4 teaspoons) active dry yeast
- 1 cup whole milk, warmed
- 1/3 cup unsalted butter, melted
- 2 large eggs
- 1 teaspoon vanilla extract
- 1/2 teaspoon salt

For the filling:

- Your choice of jam or jelly (such as raspberry, strawberry, or apricot)

For frying:

- Vegetable oil, for frying

For the topping:

- Powdered sugar, for dusting

Instructions:

1. In a large mixing bowl, combine the warm milk and granulated sugar. Sprinkle the yeast over the top and let it sit for about 5-10 minutes, or until foamy.
2. Add the melted butter, eggs, vanilla extract, and salt to the yeast mixture. Stir until well combined.
3. Gradually add the flour to the wet ingredients, mixing until a soft dough forms.
4. Turn the dough out onto a floured surface and knead for about 5-7 minutes, or until smooth and elastic.
5. Place the dough in a greased bowl, cover with a clean kitchen towel, and let it rise in a warm place for about 1 hour, or until doubled in size.
6. Once the dough has doubled in size, punch it down and turn it out onto a floured surface. Roll it out to about 1/2 inch thickness.

7. Use a round cutter or drinking glass to cut out circles of dough. Place a small spoonful of jam or jelly in the center of each circle.
8. Fold the dough over the filling and pinch the edges to seal, forming a ball.
9. Place the filled doughnuts on a baking sheet lined with parchment paper, cover with a clean kitchen towel, and let them rise for another 30 minutes.
10. Meanwhile, heat vegetable oil in a large, deep skillet or Dutch oven to 350°F (175°C).
11. Carefully add the filled doughnuts to the hot oil, frying in batches until they are golden brown on all sides, about 2-3 minutes per side.
12. Remove the Krapfen from the oil using a slotted spoon and drain them on paper towels to remove excess oil.
13. Once the Krapfen have cooled slightly, dust them generously with powdered sugar.
14. Serve the Krapfen warm and enjoy the deliciously filled and fluffy German doughnuts!

Bienenstich (Bee Sting Cake)

Ingredients:

For the dough:

- 2 and 1/4 cups all-purpose flour
- 1/4 cup granulated sugar
- 1 packet (2 and 1/4 teaspoons) active dry yeast
- 1/2 cup whole milk, warmed
- 1/4 cup unsalted butter, softened
- 1 large egg
- 1/2 teaspoon salt

For the topping:

- 1/2 cup unsalted butter
- 1/2 cup granulated sugar
- 2 tablespoons honey
- 1 and 1/2 cups sliced almonds

For the custard filling:

- 2 cups whole milk
- 1/2 cup granulated sugar
- 1/4 cup cornstarch
- 4 large egg yolks
- 1 teaspoon vanilla extract
- Pinch of salt

Instructions:

1. In a small bowl, dissolve the yeast and 1 teaspoon of sugar in the warm milk. Let it sit for about 5-10 minutes, or until foamy.
2. In a large mixing bowl, combine the flour, remaining sugar, and salt. Add the softened butter, egg, and yeast mixture. Mix until a soft dough forms.
3. Turn the dough out onto a floured surface and knead for about 5-7 minutes, or until smooth and elastic. Place the dough in a greased bowl, cover with a clean kitchen towel, and let it rise in a warm place for about 1 hour, or until doubled in size.

4. Once the dough has doubled in size, punch it down and press it evenly into a greased 9x13-inch baking pan. Let it rise again for another 30 minutes.
5. While the dough is rising, prepare the topping. In a saucepan, melt the butter over medium heat. Stir in the sugar and honey until dissolved. Remove from heat and stir in the sliced almonds.
6. Preheat your oven to 375°F (190°C). Once the dough has finished rising, spread the almond topping evenly over the dough.
7. Bake in the preheated oven for 20-25 minutes, or until the top is golden brown and caramelized. Remove from the oven and let it cool in the pan on a wire rack.
8. While the cake is cooling, prepare the custard filling. In a saucepan, heat the milk until hot but not boiling. In a separate bowl, whisk together the sugar, cornstarch, egg yolks, vanilla extract, and salt until smooth.
9. Gradually whisk the hot milk into the sugar mixture. Return the mixture to the saucepan and cook over medium heat, stirring constantly, until thickened.
10. Remove from heat and let the custard cool slightly. Once the cake has cooled, spread the custard evenly over the top.
11. Slice the Bienenstich into squares and serve. Enjoy the delicious combination of caramelized almonds, creamy custard filling, and tender dough!

Nussecken (Nut Corners)

Ingredients:

For the shortbread base:

- 1 and 1/2 cups all-purpose flour
- 1/2 cup granulated sugar
- 1/2 cup unsalted butter, softened
- 1 egg yolk
- 1 teaspoon vanilla extract
- Pinch of salt

For the nut topping:

- 1 and 1/2 cups mixed nuts (such as almonds, hazelnuts, and walnuts), finely chopped
- 1/2 cup unsalted butter
- 1/2 cup granulated sugar
- 2 tablespoons honey
- 2 tablespoons heavy cream

For assembly:

- 1/2 cup apricot jam
- 6 ounces dark chocolate, chopped (optional, for drizzling)

Instructions:

1. Preheat your oven to 350°F (175°C). Grease a 9x9-inch baking pan and line it with parchment paper, leaving some overhang for easy removal.
2. In a large mixing bowl, cream together the softened butter and granulated sugar until light and fluffy.
3. Add the egg yolk and vanilla extract, and beat until well combined.
4. Gradually add the flour and salt to the butter mixture, mixing until a dough forms.
5. Press the dough evenly into the bottom of the prepared baking pan. Bake in the preheated oven for 15-20 minutes, or until lightly golden brown. Remove from the oven and let it cool slightly.

6. While the shortbread base is cooling, prepare the nut topping. In a saucepan, melt the butter over medium heat. Stir in the sugar, honey, and heavy cream until well combined.
7. Add the finely chopped nuts to the mixture and cook, stirring constantly, for about 3-5 minutes, or until the nuts are lightly toasted and the mixture thickens slightly.
8. Spread the apricot jam evenly over the partially cooled shortbread base.
9. Spread the nut topping evenly over the apricot jam layer, pressing down gently to adhere.
10. Return the pan to the oven and bake for an additional 15-20 minutes, or until the nut topping is golden brown.
11. Remove the Nussecken from the oven and let them cool completely in the pan.
12. Once cooled, use a sharp knife to cut the Nussecken into triangles or rectangles.
13. Optional: Melt the dark chocolate in a heatproof bowl set over a pot of simmering water (double boiler). Drizzle the melted chocolate over the Nussecken for added flavor and decoration.
14. Let the chocolate set before serving. Enjoy these deliciously crunchy and nutty Nussecken as a delightful treat with your favorite hot beverage!

Pfeffernüsse (Spice Cookies)

Ingredients:

For the cookies:

- 2 cups all-purpose flour
- 1/2 cup granulated sugar
- 1/2 cup brown sugar
- 1 teaspoon baking powder
- 1/2 teaspoon baking soda
- 1/2 teaspoon ground cinnamon
- 1/2 teaspoon ground cloves
- 1/2 teaspoon ground nutmeg
- 1/2 teaspoon ground ginger
- 1/4 teaspoon ground allspice
- 1/4 teaspoon salt
- 1/2 cup unsalted butter, softened
- 1/4 cup molasses
- 1 large egg
- 1 teaspoon vanilla extract

For the coating:

- 1 cup powdered sugar

Instructions:

1. In a large mixing bowl, whisk together the flour, granulated sugar, brown sugar, baking powder, baking soda, ground cinnamon, ground cloves, ground nutmeg, ground ginger, ground allspice, and salt.
2. Add the softened butter to the dry ingredients and mix until the mixture resembles coarse crumbs.
3. In a separate bowl, whisk together the molasses, egg, and vanilla extract until well combined.
4. Gradually add the wet ingredients to the dry ingredients, mixing until a dough forms. If the dough is too sticky, you can add a little more flour.

5. Cover the dough and refrigerate it for at least 1 hour, or until firm.
6. Preheat your oven to 350°F (175°C). Line a baking sheet with parchment paper.
7. Remove the dough from the refrigerator and shape it into small balls, about 1 inch in diameter. Place the balls on the prepared baking sheet, spacing them about 2 inches apart.
8. Bake the cookies in the preheated oven for 10-12 minutes, or until set and lightly golden brown.
9. Remove the cookies from the oven and let them cool on the baking sheet for a few minutes before transferring them to a wire rack to cool completely.
10. Once the cookies are completely cool, roll them in powdered sugar until evenly coated.
11. Store the Pfeffernüsse in an airtight container at room temperature for up to one week. Enjoy these deliciously spiced cookies with a cup of tea or coffee during the holiday season or any time of the year!

Schneeballen (Snowball Cookies)

Ingredients:

- 2 cups all-purpose flour
- 1 cup unsalted butter, softened
- 1/2 cup powdered sugar, plus extra for dusting
- 1 teaspoon vanilla extract
- 1/4 teaspoon salt
- 1/2 cup finely chopped nuts (such as almonds, pecans, or walnuts) (optional)

Instructions:

1. Preheat your oven to 350°F (175°C). Line a baking sheet with parchment paper.
2. In a large mixing bowl, cream together the softened butter and powdered sugar until light and fluffy.
3. Add the vanilla extract and salt to the butter mixture and mix until well combined.
4. Gradually add the flour to the butter mixture, mixing until a dough forms. If using nuts, fold them into the dough until evenly distributed.
5. Take small portions of the dough and roll them into balls, about 1 inch in diameter, and place them on the prepared baking sheet, spacing them about 2 inches apart.
6. Bake the cookies in the preheated oven for 12-15 minutes, or until set but not browned.
7. Remove the cookies from the oven and let them cool on the baking sheet for a few minutes.
8. While the cookies are still warm, roll them in powdered sugar until evenly coated. You can do this while they are on the baking sheet or transfer them to a wire rack to cool completely and then roll them in powdered sugar.
9. Once the cookies have cooled completely and been coated in powdered sugar, they are ready to serve. Enjoy these delightful Schneeballen as a sweet treat with a cup of coffee or tea!

Streusel (Crumbles)

Ingredients:

- 1 cup all-purpose flour
- 1/2 cup granulated sugar
- 1/4 cup unsalted butter, softened
- 1/2 teaspoon ground cinnamon (optional)
- Pinch of salt

Instructions:

1. In a mixing bowl, combine the flour, sugar, cinnamon (if using), and salt.
2. Add the softened butter to the dry ingredients.
3. Use your fingers or a pastry cutter to mix the butter into the dry ingredients until the mixture resembles coarse crumbs. The mixture should hold together when pressed between your fingers, but still be crumbly.
4. Sprinkle the Streusel evenly over the top of your baked goods before baking.
5. Bake your recipe according to its instructions. The Streusel will crisp up and turn golden brown during baking.
6. Once baked, let your baked goods cool slightly before serving to allow the Streusel to set.
7. Enjoy your delicious Streusel-topped treats! They're perfect for breakfast, dessert, or any time you crave a sweet, crunchy addition to your baked goods.

Puddingteilchen (Pudding Pastries)

Ingredients:

For the pastry dough:

- 2 cups all-purpose flour
- 1/2 cup unsalted butter, cold and cubed
- 1/4 cup granulated sugar
- 1/4 teaspoon salt
- 1 large egg
- 2-3 tablespoons cold water

For the pudding filling:

- 2 cups whole milk
- 1/2 cup granulated sugar
- 1/4 cup cornstarch
- 2 large egg yolks
- 1 teaspoon vanilla extract

For the glaze (optional):

- 1 cup powdered sugar
- 1-2 tablespoons milk
- 1/2 teaspoon vanilla extract

Instructions:

1. To make the pastry dough, in a large mixing bowl, combine the flour, sugar, and salt. Add the cold, cubed butter and use a pastry cutter or your fingertips to work the butter into the flour mixture until it resembles coarse crumbs.
2. In a small bowl, whisk the egg with 2 tablespoons of cold water. Gradually add the egg mixture to the flour mixture, stirring with a fork until the dough comes together. If the dough is too dry, add an additional tablespoon of cold water as needed.

3. Shape the dough into a ball, wrap it in plastic wrap, and refrigerate for at least 30 minutes.
4. Preheat your oven to 375°F (190°C). Line a baking sheet with parchment paper.
5. On a lightly floured surface, roll out the chilled dough to about 1/4 inch thickness. Use a cookie cutter or a sharp knife to cut the dough into rectangles or squares, about 3-4 inches in size.
6. Transfer the pastry rectangles to the prepared baking sheet. Prick the surface of each pastry with a fork to prevent them from puffing up too much during baking.
7. Bake the pastries in the preheated oven for 12-15 minutes, or until golden brown. Remove from the oven and let them cool completely on a wire rack.
8. While the pastries are cooling, prepare the pudding filling. In a saucepan, heat the milk over medium heat until hot but not boiling.
9. In a separate bowl, whisk together the sugar, cornstarch, egg yolks, and vanilla extract until smooth. Gradually whisk the hot milk into the egg mixture.
10. Return the mixture to the saucepan and cook over medium heat, stirring constantly, until thickened and bubbly. Remove from heat and let the pudding cool slightly.
11. Once the pastries and pudding are cooled, use a knife to carefully slice each pastry horizontally, creating a top and bottom layer.
12. Spoon a generous amount of pudding onto the bottom half of each pastry, then place the top half back on.
13. If desired, prepare the glaze by whisking together the powdered sugar, milk, and vanilla extract until smooth. Drizzle the glaze over the top of each pastry.
14. Serve the Puddingteilchen immediately, or store them in an airtight container in the refrigerator until ready to serve. Enjoy these deliciously creamy and flaky pastries as a delightful treat with a cup of coffee or tea!

Strudel (Filled Pastry)

Ingredients:

For the dough:

- 2 cups all-purpose flour
- 1/4 teaspoon salt
- 2 tablespoons vegetable oil
- 3/4 cup lukewarm water

For the filling:

- 4 large apples, such as Granny Smith or Braeburn, peeled, cored, and thinly sliced
- 1/2 cup granulated sugar
- 1 teaspoon ground cinnamon
- 1/2 cup raisins (optional)
- 1/2 cup breadcrumbs
- 1/2 cup melted butter

For assembly:

- Powdered sugar, for dusting

Instructions:

1. Preheat your oven to 375°F (190°C). Line a baking sheet with parchment paper.
2. In a large mixing bowl, combine the flour and salt. Make a well in the center and add the vegetable oil and lukewarm water. Stir until a soft dough forms.
3. Knead the dough on a lightly floured surface for about 5-7 minutes, or until smooth and elastic. Form the dough into a ball, coat it lightly with oil, and cover it with a clean kitchen towel. Let it rest for about 30 minutes.
4. While the dough is resting, prepare the filling. In a mixing bowl, toss the sliced apples with sugar, cinnamon, and raisins (if using) until well coated.
5. Roll out the dough on a lightly floured surface into a large rectangle, about 1/8 inch thick. Brush the surface of the dough with melted butter, leaving about 1 inch border around the edges.

6. Sprinkle breadcrumbs evenly over the buttered dough, leaving the border uncovered. This will help absorb excess moisture from the filling and prevent the strudel from becoming soggy.
7. Arrange the apple filling evenly over the breadcrumbs.
8. Starting from one long edge, carefully roll the dough and filling into a log, using the parchment paper to help lift and guide the dough.
9. Place the rolled strudel seam side down on the prepared baking sheet. Brush the top with melted butter.
10. Bake in the preheated oven for 35-40 minutes, or until the strudel is golden brown and the apples are tender.
11. Remove from the oven and let the strudel cool slightly on the baking sheet.
12. Dust the strudel with powdered sugar before serving.
13. Slice the strudel and serve warm or at room temperature. Enjoy the sweet and flaky goodness of homemade apple strudel!

Honigkuchen (Honey Cake)

Ingredients:

For the cake:

- 2 cups all-purpose flour
- 1 teaspoon baking powder
- 1/2 teaspoon baking soda
- 1 teaspoon ground cinnamon
- 1/2 teaspoon ground ginger
- 1/4 teaspoon ground cloves
- 1/4 teaspoon ground nutmeg
- 1/2 cup unsalted butter, softened
- 1 cup granulated sugar
- 3 large eggs
- 1 cup honey
- 1/2 cup strong brewed coffee, cooled
- 1/4 cup milk

For the glaze:

- 1 cup powdered sugar
- 2-3 tablespoons milk
- 1 teaspoon vanilla extract

Instructions:

1. Preheat your oven to 350°F (175°C). Grease and flour a 9x5-inch loaf pan.
2. In a medium mixing bowl, whisk together the flour, baking powder, baking soda, cinnamon, ginger, cloves, and nutmeg.
3. In a large mixing bowl, cream together the softened butter and granulated sugar until light and fluffy.
4. Add the eggs, one at a time, beating well after each addition.
5. Stir in the honey, brewed coffee, and milk until well combined.
6. Gradually add the dry ingredients to the wet ingredients, mixing until just combined and no lumps remain.

7. Pour the batter into the prepared loaf pan and spread it out evenly.
8. Bake in the preheated oven for 45-50 minutes, or until a toothpick inserted into the center comes out clean.
9. Remove the cake from the oven and let it cool in the pan for 10 minutes before transferring it to a wire rack to cool completely.
10. While the cake is cooling, prepare the glaze. In a small mixing bowl, whisk together the powdered sugar, milk, and vanilla extract until smooth. Adjust the consistency by adding more milk if needed.
11. Once the cake has cooled completely, drizzle the glaze over the top.
12. Let the glaze set before slicing and serving the Honigkuchen. Enjoy the rich, moist, and flavorful Honey Cake as a delightful treat with a cup of tea or coffee!

Käsekuchen (Cheesecake)

Ingredients:

For the crust:

- 1 and 1/2 cups graham cracker crumbs (about 10-12 whole graham crackers)
- 1/4 cup granulated sugar
- 1/2 cup unsalted butter, melted

For the filling:

- 24 ounces (3 packages) cream cheese, softened
- 1 cup granulated sugar
- 1 teaspoon vanilla extract
- 4 large eggs
- 1/4 cup sour cream
- 1/4 cup all-purpose flour
- Zest of 1 lemon (optional)

For the topping (optional):

- 1 cup sour cream
- 2 tablespoons granulated sugar
- 1 teaspoon vanilla extract

Instructions:

1. Preheat your oven to 325°F (160°C). Grease a 9-inch springform pan.
2. In a mixing bowl, combine the graham cracker crumbs, sugar, and melted butter until the mixture resembles wet sand.
3. Press the mixture into the bottom of the prepared springform pan, forming an even layer. Use the bottom of a flat glass or measuring cup to help press it down firmly.
4. Bake the crust in the preheated oven for 10 minutes. Remove from the oven and let it cool while you prepare the filling.

5. In a large mixing bowl, beat the softened cream cheese, sugar, and vanilla extract until smooth and creamy.
6. Add the eggs one at a time, mixing well after each addition.
7. Stir in the sour cream, flour, and lemon zest (if using) until well combined.
8. Pour the filling over the cooled crust in the springform pan, spreading it out evenly.
9. Bake the cheesecake in the preheated oven for 50-60 minutes, or until the edges are set but the center still jiggles slightly when shaken.
10. While the cheesecake is baking, prepare the optional topping by mixing together the sour cream, sugar, and vanilla extract.
11. After the cheesecake has finished baking, remove it from the oven and carefully spread the topping over the hot cheesecake.
12. Return the cheesecake to the oven and bake for an additional 10 minutes.
13. Turn off the oven and leave the cheesecake inside with the door slightly ajar for about 1 hour to cool gradually.
14. Remove the cheesecake from the oven and run a knife around the edges to loosen it from the pan. Allow it to cool completely before refrigerating for at least 4 hours or overnight.
15. Once chilled, slice and serve the Käsekuchen. Enjoy the creamy and decadent delight of homemade German cheesecake!

Mandelhörnchen (Almond Crescents)

Ingredients:

For the dough:

- 2 cups almond meal (ground almonds)
- 1 cup powdered sugar
- 2 large egg whites
- 1 teaspoon almond extract
- Pinch of salt

For the coating:

- 1 cup powdered sugar
- 1/2 cup sliced almonds

Instructions:

1. Preheat your oven to 325°F (160°C). Line a baking sheet with parchment paper.
2. In a large mixing bowl, combine the almond meal, powdered sugar, almond extract, and salt.
3. In a separate bowl, beat the egg whites until stiff peaks form.
4. Gently fold the beaten egg whites into the almond mixture until well combined. The dough should be moist and hold together.
5. Take small portions of the dough and shape them into crescent moons, about 2-3 inches long, and place them on the prepared baking sheet.
6. Bake the Mandelhörnchen in the preheated oven for 15-18 minutes, or until they are set and lightly golden brown.
7. While the Mandelhörnchen are baking, prepare the coating. Place the sliced almonds on a baking sheet and toast them in the oven for 5-7 minutes, or until lightly golden brown. Remove from the oven and let them cool.
8. Once the Mandelhörnchen are baked, let them cool on the baking sheet for a few minutes before transferring them to a wire rack to cool completely.
9. Once cooled, dip each Mandelhörnchen into powdered sugar to coat them generously.

10. Sprinkle the toasted sliced almonds over the powdered sugar coating, pressing them gently to adhere.
11. Let the Mandelhörnchen sit for a few minutes to allow the coating to set before serving.
12. Enjoy these deliciously nutty and sweet Almond Crescents with a cup of coffee or tea for a delightful treat!

Eclairs (Cream-Filled Pastries)

Ingredients:

For the choux pastry:

- 1/2 cup water
- 1/2 cup whole milk
- 1/2 cup unsalted butter
- 1 tablespoon granulated sugar
- 1/4 teaspoon salt
- 1 cup all-purpose flour
- 4 large eggs

For the pastry cream filling:

- 2 cups whole milk
- 1/2 cup granulated sugar
- 4 large egg yolks
- 1/4 cup cornstarch
- 1 teaspoon vanilla extract

For the chocolate icing:

- 4 ounces semi-sweet chocolate, chopped
- 1/2 cup heavy cream
- 1 tablespoon unsalted butter

Instructions:

1. Preheat your oven to 400°F (200°C). Line a baking sheet with parchment paper.
2. In a medium saucepan, combine the water, milk, butter, sugar, and salt. Bring to a boil over medium heat.
3. Once the mixture is boiling, add the flour all at once and stir vigorously with a wooden spoon until the mixture forms a ball and pulls away from the sides of the pan.
4. Transfer the dough to a mixing bowl and let it cool for a few minutes.

5. Add the eggs, one at a time, beating well after each addition, until the dough is smooth and glossy.
6. Transfer the dough to a piping bag fitted with a large round tip. Pipe the dough onto the prepared baking sheet into 4-inch-long strips, leaving space between each eclair.
7. Bake in the preheated oven for 25-30 minutes, or until the eclairs are golden brown and puffed up. Reduce the oven temperature to 350°F (175°C) halfway through baking.
8. Remove the eclairs from the oven and let them cool completely on a wire rack.
9. While the eclairs are cooling, prepare the pastry cream filling. In a saucepan, heat the milk over medium heat until hot but not boiling.
10. In a separate bowl, whisk together the sugar, egg yolks, and cornstarch until smooth and pale yellow.
11. Gradually whisk the hot milk into the egg mixture. Return the mixture to the saucepan and cook over medium heat, stirring constantly, until thickened.
12. Remove from heat and stir in the vanilla extract. Transfer the pastry cream to a bowl and cover it with plastic wrap, pressing the wrap directly onto the surface to prevent a skin from forming. Let it cool completely.
13. Once the eclairs and pastry cream are cooled, use a sharp knife to make a small slit in the side of each eclair.
14. Transfer the pastry cream to a piping bag fitted with a small round tip. Pipe the cream into each eclair through the slit.
15. For the chocolate icing, place the chopped chocolate and butter in a heatproof bowl. In a small saucepan, heat the heavy cream until it just begins to simmer. Pour the hot cream over the chocolate and let it sit for a minute. Stir until smooth and glossy.
16. Dip the top of each eclair into the chocolate icing, letting any excess drip off. Place the eclairs on a wire rack to set the icing.
17. Serve the eclairs immediately, or store them in the refrigerator until ready to serve. Enjoy these classic cream-filled pastries as a decadent treat!

Baumkuchen (Tree Cake)

Ingredients:

For the batter:

- 1 cup unsalted butter, softened
- 1 cup granulated sugar
- 6 large eggs
- 1 teaspoon vanilla extract
- 1 cup all-purpose flour
- 1/2 cup cornstarch
- 1/4 teaspoon salt
- 1/4 cup milk

For the glaze:

- 1 cup powdered sugar
- 2-3 tablespoons milk
- 1/2 teaspoon vanilla extract

Instructions:

1. Preheat your oven to broil or use a grill if you have one. Grease a 9-inch round cake pan and line the bottom with parchment paper.
2. In a large mixing bowl, cream together the softened butter and granulated sugar until light and fluffy.
3. Add the eggs, one at a time, beating well after each addition. Stir in the vanilla extract.
4. In a separate bowl, sift together the flour, cornstarch, and salt.
5. Gradually add the dry ingredients to the wet ingredients, alternating with the milk, and mix until a smooth batter forms.
6. Pour a thin layer of batter into the prepared cake pan and spread it out evenly.
7. Place the cake pan under the broiler or on the grill for a few minutes until the batter is set and lightly golden brown.

8. Remove the pan from the broiler or grill and carefully pour another thin layer of batter over the cooked layer. Return it to the broiler or grill and repeat this process until all the batter is used, creating multiple layers.
9. Once all the layers are cooked, remove the cake from the oven or grill and let it cool in the pan for a few minutes before transferring it to a wire rack to cool completely.
10. While the cake is cooling, prepare the glaze by whisking together the powdered sugar, milk, and vanilla extract until smooth. Adjust the consistency by adding more milk if needed.
11. Once the cake is completely cool, drizzle the glaze over the top of the Baumkuchen.
12. Let the glaze set before slicing and serving the cake. Enjoy the unique and delicious Baumkuchen with a cup of coffee or tea for a special treat!

Kuchen (Cakes)

Ingredients:

- 1 cup all-purpose flour
- 1 teaspoon baking powder
- Pinch of salt
- 4 large eggs, at room temperature
- 1 cup granulated sugar
- 1 teaspoon vanilla extract
- 1/2 cup unsalted butter, melted and cooled
- 1/4 cup milk

Instructions:

1. Preheat your oven to 350°F (175°C). Grease and flour a 9-inch round cake pan or line it with parchment paper.
2. In a medium bowl, sift together the flour, baking powder, and salt. Set aside.
3. In a large mixing bowl, beat the eggs and granulated sugar together with an electric mixer on high speed until pale and fluffy, about 5 minutes.
4. Beat in the vanilla extract until combined.
5. Gradually add the melted butter to the egg mixture, beating on low speed until well incorporated.
6. Alternately add the flour mixture and milk to the batter in three additions, beginning and ending with the flour mixture. Mix until just combined after each addition, being careful not to overmix.
7. Pour the batter into the prepared cake pan and spread it out evenly.
8. Bake in the preheated oven for 25-30 minutes, or until a toothpick inserted into the center of the cake comes out clean.
9. Remove the cake from the oven and let it cool in the pan for 10 minutes before transferring it to a wire rack to cool completely.
10. Once the cake is cooled, it can be served plain or decorated with your choice of frosting, glaze, fruit, whipped cream, or other toppings.
11. Slice and serve the cake, and enjoy your homemade German-style Kuchen!

Feel free to experiment with different flavorings, fillings, and decorations to create your own unique variations of Kuchen.

Plätzchen (Cookies)

Ingredients:

- 2 cups all-purpose flour
- 1/2 teaspoon baking powder
- 1/4 teaspoon salt
- 1/2 cup granulated sugar
- 1 large egg
- 1 teaspoon vanilla extract
- 1 cup unsalted butter, softened
- Optional: Additional granulated sugar for sprinkling, colored sugar, or decorative sprinkles

Instructions:

1. Preheat your oven to 350°F (175°C). Line a baking sheet with parchment paper.
2. In a medium bowl, whisk together the flour, baking powder, and salt. Set aside.
3. In a large mixing bowl, cream together the softened butter and granulated sugar until light and fluffy.
4. Add the egg and vanilla extract to the butter mixture, and beat until well combined.
5. Gradually add the flour mixture to the butter mixture, mixing until a smooth dough forms. If the dough is too sticky, you can add a little more flour.
6. Roll out the dough on a lightly floured surface to about 1/4 inch thickness.
7. Use cookie cutters to cut out shapes from the dough and place them on the prepared baking sheet, spacing them about 1 inch apart.
8. If desired, sprinkle the cookies with additional granulated sugar, colored sugar, or decorative sprinkles.
9. Bake the cookies in the preheated oven for 10-12 minutes, or until the edges are lightly golden brown.
10. Remove the cookies from the oven and let them cool on the baking sheet for a few minutes before transferring them to a wire rack to cool completely.
11. Once cooled, the Butterplätzchen are ready to be enjoyed! Store them in an airtight container at room temperature for up to one week.

Feel free to get creative with your Butterplätzchen by using different cookie cutter shapes and decorations. Enjoy these classic German butter cookies with a cup of tea or coffee for a delightful treat!

Kirschkuchen (Cherry Cake)

Ingredients:

For the cake:

- 1 and 1/2 cups all-purpose flour
- 1 and 1/2 teaspoons baking powder
- 1/4 teaspoon salt
- 1/2 cup unsalted butter, softened
- 3/4 cup granulated sugar
- 2 large eggs
- 1 teaspoon vanilla extract
- 1/2 cup milk

For the cherry topping:

- 2 cups fresh cherries, pitted and halved
- 1/4 cup granulated sugar
- 1 tablespoon cornstarch

For the crumb topping (optional):

- 1/4 cup all-purpose flour
- 1/4 cup granulated sugar
- 2 tablespoons unsalted butter, melted

Instructions:

1. Preheat your oven to 350°F (175°C). Grease and flour a 9-inch round cake pan or line it with parchment paper.
2. In a medium bowl, whisk together the flour, baking powder, and salt. Set aside.
3. In a large mixing bowl, cream together the softened butter and granulated sugar until light and fluffy.
4. Add the eggs, one at a time, beating well after each addition. Stir in the vanilla extract.
5. Gradually add the dry ingredients to the wet ingredients, alternating with the milk and mix until just combined.
6. Pour the batter into the prepared cake pan and spread it out evenly.

7. In a separate bowl, toss the halved cherries with the sugar and cornstarch until well coated.
8. Arrange the cherry mixture evenly over the top of the cake batter.
9. If using the crumb topping, combine the flour, sugar, and melted butter in a small bowl. Sprinkle the crumb topping over the cherries.
10. Bake the cake in the preheated oven for 35-40 minutes, or until a toothpick inserted into the center comes out clean.
11. Remove the cake from the oven and let it cool in the pan for 10 minutes before transferring it to a wire rack to cool completely.
12. Once cooled, slice and serve the Kirschkuchen. Enjoy the delicious combination of moist cake and sweet cherries as a delightful dessert or afternoon treat!

Feel free to customize this recipe by using different fruits or adding a scoop of whipped cream or a dollop of vanilla ice cream on top of each slice.

Rhabarberkuchen (Rhubarb Cake)

Ingredients:

For the cake:

- 2 cups all-purpose flour
- 1 and 1/2 teaspoons baking powder
- 1/2 teaspoon salt
- 1/2 cup unsalted butter, softened
- 1 cup granulated sugar
- 2 large eggs
- 1 teaspoon vanilla extract
- 1/2 cup sour cream or Greek yogurt
- 2 cups chopped rhubarb (fresh or frozen)

For the streusel topping:

- 1/4 cup all-purpose flour
- 1/4 cup granulated sugar
- 2 tablespoons unsalted butter, cold

Instructions:

1. Preheat your oven to 350°F (175°C). Grease and flour a 9x13-inch baking dish or line it with parchment paper.
2. In a medium bowl, whisk together the flour, baking powder, and salt. Set aside.
3. In a large mixing bowl, cream together the softened butter and granulated sugar until light and fluffy.
4. Add the eggs, one at a time, beating well after each addition. Stir in the vanilla extract.
5. Gradually add the dry ingredients to the wet ingredients, alternating with the sour cream or Greek yogurt, and mix until just combined.
6. Gently fold in the chopped rhubarb until evenly distributed throughout the batter.
7. Spread the batter evenly into the prepared baking dish.

8. To make the streusel topping, combine the flour and sugar in a small bowl. Cut in the cold butter using a pastry cutter or your fingers until the mixture resembles coarse crumbs. Sprinkle the streusel evenly over the top of the cake batter.
9. Bake the cake in the preheated oven for 35-40 minutes, or until a toothpick inserted into the center comes out clean and the top is lightly golden brown.
10. Remove the cake from the oven and let it cool in the pan for 10 minutes before transferring it to a wire rack to cool completely.
11. Once cooled, slice and serve the Rhabarberkuchen. Enjoy the perfect balance of sweet cake and tart rhubarb in every bite!

Feel free to dust the cake with powdered sugar before serving for an extra touch of sweetness. This cake is best enjoyed fresh but can be stored in an airtight container at room temperature for a few days.

Mürbeteig (Shortcrust Pastry)

Ingredients:

- 2 cups all-purpose flour
- 1/2 cup granulated sugar (for sweet pastry) OR 1/2 teaspoon salt (for savory pastry)
- 1 cup unsalted butter, cold and cut into small cubes
- 1 large egg
- 1-2 tablespoons ice water (if needed)

Instructions:

1. In a large mixing bowl, combine the flour and sugar (for sweet pastry) OR salt (for savory pastry).
2. Add the cold, cubed butter to the flour mixture.
3. Use a pastry cutter, two knives, or your fingertips to work the butter into the flour until the mixture resembles coarse crumbs. The butter should be evenly distributed throughout the flour, with no large chunks remaining.
4. In a small bowl, lightly beat the egg.
5. Gradually add the beaten egg to the flour mixture, mixing with a fork or your hands until the dough begins to come together. If the dough seems too dry and crumbly, add ice water, one tablespoon at a time, until the dough holds together when pressed.
6. Gather the dough into a ball and flatten it into a disk. Wrap it in plastic wrap and refrigerate for at least 30 minutes to allow the butter to firm up and the gluten to relax.
7. Once chilled, remove the dough from the refrigerator and let it sit at room temperature for a few minutes to soften slightly.
8. On a lightly floured surface, roll out the dough to the desired thickness, depending on your recipe. For a tart or pie crust, aim for about 1/8 to 1/4 inch thickness.
9. Carefully transfer the rolled-out dough to your tart or pie pan, pressing it gently into the bottom and up the sides. Trim any excess dough and crimp the edges if desired.
10. Depending on your recipe, you may need to blind bake (pre-bake) the crust before adding the filling. Follow your recipe instructions for baking times and temperatures.

11. Once baked, let the Mürbeteig cool completely before filling or serving according to your recipe.

Enjoy your homemade Mürbeteig as the base for delicious sweet or savory treats!

Hefezopf (Yeast Braid)

Ingredients:

For the dough:

- 4 cups all-purpose flour
- 1/2 cup granulated sugar
- 2 and 1/4 teaspoons (1 packet) active dry yeast
- 1 teaspoon salt
- 1/2 cup unsalted butter, melted
- 1 cup warm milk (about 110°F/45°C)
- 2 large eggs, beaten
- 1 teaspoon vanilla extract
- Zest of 1 lemon (optional)

For the egg wash:

- 1 large egg
- 1 tablespoon milk

Instructions:

1. In a large mixing bowl, combine 2 cups of flour, sugar, yeast, and salt. Stir to combine.
2. Add the melted butter, warm milk, beaten eggs, vanilla extract, and lemon zest (if using) to the dry ingredients. Mix until well combined.
3. Gradually add the remaining flour, 1/2 cup at a time, until a soft dough forms. You may not need to use all of the flour.
4. Turn the dough out onto a lightly floured surface and knead for 8-10 minutes, or until the dough is smooth and elastic.
5. Place the dough in a greased bowl, turning once to coat. Cover with a clean kitchen towel or plastic wrap and let it rise in a warm, draft-free place for 1-1.5 hours, or until doubled in size.
6. Once the dough has doubled in size, punch it down to release the air bubbles. Divide the dough into three equal portions.
7. Roll each portion into a long rope, about 20-24 inches (50-60 cm) long.

8. Place the three ropes side by side on a greased baking sheet. Pinch the tops together and braid the ropes together, tucking the ends underneath.
9. Cover the braided loaf with a clean kitchen towel and let it rise for another 30-45 minutes, or until puffy.
10. Preheat your oven to 350°F (175°C).
11. In a small bowl, whisk together the egg and milk to make the egg wash. Brush the egg wash over the top of the braided loaf.
12. Bake the Hefezopf in the preheated oven for 25-30 minutes, or until golden brown and cooked through.
13. Remove from the oven and let it cool on a wire rack before slicing and serving.

Enjoy your homemade Hefezopf warm or at room temperature, sliced and served with butter or your favorite jam. It's perfect for breakfast, brunch, or as a sweet treat any time of day!

Franzbrötchen (Cinnamon Pastries)

Ingredients:

For the dough:

- 2 and 1/4 cups all-purpose flour
- 1/4 cup granulated sugar
- 1/2 teaspoon salt
- 1 packet (2 and 1/4 teaspoons) active dry yeast
- 1/2 cup warm milk (about 110°F/45°C)
- 1/4 cup unsalted butter, melted
- 1 large egg

For the filling:

- 1/2 cup unsalted butter, softened
- 1/2 cup granulated sugar
- 2 tablespoons ground cinnamon

For the topping:

- 1 large egg, beaten (for egg wash)
- Pearl sugar (optional, for topping)

Instructions:

1. In a large mixing bowl, combine the flour, sugar, salt, and active dry yeast.
2. In a separate bowl, whisk together the warm milk, melted butter, and egg.
3. Pour the wet ingredients into the dry ingredients and mix until a dough forms.
4. Turn the dough out onto a lightly floured surface and knead for about 5-7 minutes, or until the dough is smooth and elastic.
5. Place the dough in a greased bowl, cover with a clean kitchen towel or plastic wrap, and let it rise in a warm, draft-free place for about 1 hour, or until doubled in size.
6. While the dough is rising, prepare the filling by mixing together the softened butter, sugar, and ground cinnamon until well combined. Set aside.
7. Once the dough has doubled in size, punch it down to release the air bubbles. Roll out the dough on a lightly floured surface into a rectangle, about 1/4 inch thick.

8. Spread the cinnamon filling evenly over the surface of the dough.
9. Starting from one long edge, tightly roll up the dough into a log.
10. Using a sharp knife, slice the log into equal-sized pieces, about 1 inch wide.
11. Place the sliced pieces onto a parchment-lined baking sheet, leaving some space between each one.
12. Cover the Franzbrötchen with a clean kitchen towel and let them rise for another 30-45 minutes, or until puffy.
13. Preheat your oven to 375°F (190°C).
14. Brush the risen Franzbrötchen with beaten egg and sprinkle them with pearl sugar, if desired.
15. Bake in the preheated oven for 15-18 minutes, or until golden brown and cooked through.
16. Remove from the oven and let them cool on a wire rack before serving.

Enjoy your homemade Franzbrötchen warm or at room temperature. They are perfect for breakfast or as a sweet treat with a cup of coffee or tea!

Aprikosenkuchen (Apricot Cake)

Ingredients:

For the cake:

- 1 and 1/2 cups all-purpose flour
- 1 and 1/2 teaspoons baking powder
- 1/4 teaspoon salt
- 1/2 cup unsalted butter, softened
- 3/4 cup granulated sugar
- 2 large eggs
- 1 teaspoon vanilla extract
- 1/3 cup milk

For the apricot topping:

- 1 pound fresh apricots, halved and pitted
- 2 tablespoons granulated sugar
- 1 tablespoon lemon juice
- 2 tablespoons apricot jam or preserves

Instructions:

1. Preheat your oven to 350°F (175°C). Grease and flour a 9-inch round cake pan or line it with parchment paper.
2. In a medium bowl, whisk together the flour, baking powder, and salt. Set aside.
3. In a large mixing bowl, cream together the softened butter and granulated sugar until light and fluffy.
4. Add the eggs, one at a time, beating well after each addition. Stir in the vanilla extract.
5. Gradually add the dry ingredients to the wet ingredients, alternating with the milk, and mix until just combined.
6. Spread the cake batter evenly into the prepared cake pan.
7. Arrange the apricot halves, cut side up, on top of the cake batter in a single layer, slightly overlapping them.

8. In a small bowl, mix together the granulated sugar and lemon juice. Drizzle the mixture over the apricots.
9. Bake the cake in the preheated oven for 30-35 minutes, or until a toothpick inserted into the center comes out clean and the top is lightly golden brown.
10. Remove the cake from the oven and let it cool in the pan for 10 minutes.
11. Warm the apricot jam or preserves in a small saucepan over low heat until melted and smooth. Brush the melted jam over the top of the warm cake.
12. Allow the cake to cool completely in the pan before slicing and serving.

Enjoy your homemade Aprikosenkuchen with a dollop of whipped cream or a scoop of vanilla ice cream for a deliciously fruity dessert!

Eierschecke (Layered Cake)

Ingredients:

For the shortcrust pastry base:

- 1 and 1/2 cups all-purpose flour
- 1/2 cup granulated sugar
- 1/2 cup unsalted butter, cold and cubed
- 1 large egg
- Pinch of salt

For the quark filling:

- 1 and 1/2 cups quark (or substitute with cream cheese or ricotta cheese)
- 1/2 cup granulated sugar
- 2 large eggs
- 1 teaspoon vanilla extract
- Zest of 1 lemon
- 1 tablespoon cornstarch

For the sponge cake topping:

- 2 large eggs
- 1/2 cup granulated sugar
- 1/2 cup all-purpose flour
- 1/2 teaspoon baking powder

Instructions:

1. Preheat your oven to 350°F (175°C). Grease and flour a 9x13-inch baking dish or line it with parchment paper.
2. In a large mixing bowl, combine the flour, sugar, and salt for the shortcrust pastry base.
3. Add the cold, cubed butter to the flour mixture. Use your fingertips or a pastry cutter to work the butter into the flour until the mixture resembles coarse crumbs.

4. Add the egg to the flour mixture and mix until a dough forms. Press the dough evenly into the bottom of the prepared baking dish.
5. In another mixing bowl, prepare the quark filling by whisking together the quark, sugar, eggs, vanilla extract, lemon zest, and cornstarch until smooth and well combined.
6. Pour the quark filling over the shortcrust pastry base, spreading it out evenly.
7. In a separate mixing bowl, prepare the sponge cake topping by whisking together the eggs and sugar until light and fluffy.
8. Gradually add the flour and baking powder to the egg mixture, folding gently until just combined.
9. Pour the sponge cake batter over the quark filling, spreading it out evenly.
10. Bake in the preheated oven for 25-30 minutes, or until the top is golden brown and the cake is set.
11. Remove from the oven and let the Eierschecke cool completely in the baking dish.
12. Once cooled, slice the Eierschecke into squares and serve. Enjoy the delicious layers of this traditional German cake!

You can also dust the top with powdered sugar before serving for an extra touch of sweetness. Eierschecke is best enjoyed fresh, but leftovers can be stored in an airtight container in the refrigerator for a few days.

Schokoladentorte (Chocolate Cake)

Ingredients:

For the cake:

- 1 and 3/4 cups all-purpose flour
- 3/4 cup unsweetened cocoa powder
- 1 and 3/4 cups granulated sugar
- 1 and 1/2 teaspoons baking powder
- 1 and 1/2 teaspoons baking soda
- 1 teaspoon salt
- 2 large eggs
- 1 cup buttermilk
- 1/2 cup vegetable oil
- 2 teaspoons vanilla extract
- 1 cup boiling water

For the chocolate ganache frosting:

- 1 cup heavy cream
- 8 ounces semi-sweet chocolate, finely chopped
- 1 tablespoon unsalted butter

Instructions:

1. Preheat your oven to 350°F (175°C). Grease and flour two 9-inch round cake pans or line them with parchment paper.
2. In a large mixing bowl, sift together the flour, cocoa powder, granulated sugar, baking powder, baking soda, and salt.
3. Add the eggs, buttermilk, vegetable oil, and vanilla extract to the dry ingredients. Mix on medium speed until well combined, about 2 minutes.
4. Reduce the mixer speed to low and carefully add the boiling water to the batter. Mix until just combined. The batter will be thin.
5. Divide the batter evenly between the prepared cake pans.
6. Bake in the preheated oven for 30-35 minutes, or until a toothpick inserted into the center of the cakes comes out clean.

7. Remove the cakes from the oven and let them cool in the pans for 10 minutes before transferring them to a wire rack to cool completely.
8. While the cakes are cooling, prepare the chocolate ganache frosting. In a small saucepan, heat the heavy cream over medium heat until it just begins to simmer.
9. Place the chopped chocolate in a heatproof bowl. Pour the hot cream over the chocolate and let it sit for 1-2 minutes.
10. Add the butter to the chocolate mixture and stir until smooth and glossy.
11. Let the ganache cool to room temperature, stirring occasionally, until it thickens to a spreadable consistency.
12. Once the cakes are completely cool and the ganache has thickened, assemble the cake by placing one cake layer on a serving plate or cake stand. Spread a layer of ganache evenly over the top of the cake layer.
13. Place the second cake layer on top and spread the remaining ganache over the top and sides of the cake.
14. Optionally, decorate the cake with chocolate shavings, sprinkles, or fresh berries.
15. Chill the cake in the refrigerator for at least 30 minutes to allow the ganache to set before slicing and serving.

Enjoy your homemade Schokoladentorte with a tall glass of cold milk or a cup of hot coffee for a truly indulgent treat!

Erdbeerkuchen (Strawberry Cake)

Ingredients:

For the cake:

- 1 and 1/2 cups all-purpose flour
- 1 and 1/2 teaspoons baking powder
- 1/4 teaspoon salt
- 1/2 cup unsalted butter, softened
- 1 cup granulated sugar
- 2 large eggs
- 1 teaspoon vanilla extract
- 1/2 cup milk

For the strawberry filling:

- 2 cups fresh strawberries, hulled and sliced
- 1/4 cup granulated sugar
- 1 tablespoon cornstarch
- 1 tablespoon lemon juice

For the whipped cream topping:

- 1 cup heavy cream, chilled
- 2 tablespoons powdered sugar
- 1 teaspoon vanilla extract

For garnish:

- Additional fresh strawberries, whole or sliced

Instructions:

1. Preheat your oven to 350°F (175°C). Grease and flour a 9-inch round cake pan or line it with parchment paper.
2. In a medium bowl, whisk together the flour, baking powder, and salt. Set aside.
3. In a large mixing bowl, cream together the softened butter and granulated sugar until light and fluffy.

4. Add the eggs, one at a time, beating well after each addition. Stir in the vanilla extract.
5. Gradually add the dry ingredients to the wet ingredients, alternating with the milk, and mix until just combined.
6. Pour the cake batter into the prepared cake pan and spread it out evenly.
7. Bake in the preheated oven for 25-30 minutes, or until a toothpick inserted into the center comes out clean and the top is lightly golden brown.
8. Remove the cake from the oven and let it cool in the pan for 10 minutes before transferring it to a wire rack to cool completely.
9. While the cake is cooling, prepare the strawberry filling. In a medium saucepan, combine the sliced strawberries, granulated sugar, cornstarch, and lemon juice. Cook over medium heat, stirring occasionally, until the strawberries release their juices and the mixture thickens slightly, about 5-7 minutes. Remove from heat and let it cool completely.
10. In a chilled mixing bowl, beat the heavy cream, powdered sugar, and vanilla extract until stiff peaks form to make the whipped cream topping.
11. Once the cake and strawberry filling are completely cooled, spread the strawberry filling over the top of the cake.
12. Dollop the whipped cream topping over the strawberry filling and spread it out evenly.
13. Garnish the cake with additional fresh strawberries, whole or sliced, as desired.
14. Chill the cake in the refrigerator for at least 1 hour before slicing and serving to allow the flavors to meld together.

Enjoy your homemade Erdbeerkuchen with its luscious layers of cake, fresh strawberries, and whipped cream for a delightful summer treat!

Butterkuchen (Butter Cake)

Ingredients:

For the dough:

- 2 and 1/4 cups all-purpose flour
- 1/4 cup granulated sugar
- 1 packet (2 and 1/4 teaspoons) active dry yeast
- 1/2 teaspoon salt
- 1/2 cup warm milk (about 110°F/45°C)
- 1/4 cup unsalted butter, melted
- 1 large egg

For the topping:

- 1/2 cup unsalted butter, softened
- 1/2 cup granulated sugar
- 1 teaspoon vanilla extract
- 1/4 teaspoon almond extract (optional)
- 1/4 teaspoon ground cinnamon
- Sliced almonds for garnish (optional)

Instructions:

1. In a large mixing bowl, combine the flour, sugar, yeast, and salt for the dough.
2. Add the warm milk, melted butter, and egg to the dry ingredients. Mix until a dough forms.
3. Turn the dough out onto a lightly floured surface and knead for about 5-7 minutes, or until the dough is smooth and elastic.
4. Place the dough in a greased bowl, cover with a clean kitchen towel or plastic wrap, and let it rise in a warm, draft-free place for about 1 hour, or until doubled in size.
5. Once the dough has doubled in size, punch it down to release the air bubbles. Press the dough evenly into the bottom of a greased 9x13-inch baking dish.
6. In a small mixing bowl, cream together the softened butter, sugar, vanilla extract, almond extract (if using), and ground cinnamon for the topping.

7. Spread the butter mixture evenly over the top of the dough in the baking dish.
8. If desired, sprinkle sliced almonds over the top of the butter mixture for garnish.
9. Cover the baking dish with a clean kitchen towel and let it rise for another 30-45 minutes, or until puffy.
10. Preheat your oven to 375°F (190°C).
11. Bake the Butterkuchen in the preheated oven for 20-25 minutes, or until golden brown and cooked through.
12. Remove from the oven and let it cool slightly before slicing and serving.

Enjoy your homemade Butterkuchen warm or at room temperature. It's perfect for breakfast, brunch, or as a sweet treat with a cup of coffee or tea!

Vanillekipferl (Vanilla Crescents)

Ingredients:

- 1 cup unsalted butter, softened
- 2/3 cup granulated sugar
- 1 and 1/2 cups ground almonds
- 2 cups all-purpose flour
- 1 teaspoon vanilla extract
- Pinch of salt
- 1 cup powdered sugar, for coating
- 2 tablespoons vanilla sugar, for coating

Instructions:

1. In a large mixing bowl, cream together the softened butter and granulated sugar until light and fluffy.
2. Add the ground almonds, flour, vanilla extract, and salt to the butter mixture. Mix until a dough forms.
3. Divide the dough into two equal portions. Shape each portion into a disk, wrap them in plastic wrap, and chill in the refrigerator for at least 30 minutes.
4. Preheat your oven to 350°F (175°C). Line a baking sheet with parchment paper.
5. Remove one disk of dough from the refrigerator. Pinch off small pieces of dough and roll them into small logs, about 2 inches long.
6. Shape each log into a crescent moon shape and place them on the prepared baking sheet, spacing them about 1 inch apart.
7. Bake the Vanillekipferl in the preheated oven for 10-12 minutes, or until lightly golden brown.
8. While the cookies are still warm, carefully transfer them to a wire rack to cool slightly.
9. In a shallow bowl, mix together the powdered sugar and vanilla sugar for coating.
10. Once the cookies have cooled slightly but are still warm to the touch, gently roll them in the powdered sugar mixture to coat them evenly.
11. Place the coated Vanillekipferl on a wire rack to cool completely.
12. Once cooled, store the cookies in an airtight container at room temperature. They will keep for several days.

Enjoy your homemade Vanillekipferl with a cup of tea or coffee for a deliciously festive treat during the holiday season!

Kokosmakronen (Coconut Macaroons)

Ingredients:

- 3 large egg whites
- 1 cup granulated sugar
- 1 teaspoon vanilla extract
- 3 cups shredded coconut (unsweetened)
- Optional: 1/4 teaspoon almond extract (for extra flavor)

Instructions:

1. Preheat your oven to 325°F (160°C). Line a baking sheet with parchment paper or a silicone baking mat.
2. In a clean, dry mixing bowl, beat the egg whites with an electric mixer on medium-high speed until stiff peaks form.
3. Gradually add the granulated sugar, a little at a time, while continuing to beat the egg whites until they are glossy and hold stiff peaks.
4. Beat in the vanilla extract (and almond extract if using) until well combined.
5. Gently fold in the shredded coconut using a spatula until evenly distributed and the mixture is well combined.
6. Using a spoon or cookie scoop, drop rounded tablespoons of the coconut mixture onto the prepared baking sheet, spacing them about 1 inch apart.
7. Optionally, use your fingers to shape the mounds into smooth, rounded domes.
8. Bake in the preheated oven for 15-18 minutes, or until the coconut macaroons are lightly golden brown around the edges.
9. Remove from the oven and let the macaroons cool on the baking sheet for a few minutes before transferring them to a wire rack to cool completely.
10. Once cooled, store the Kokosmakronen in an airtight container at room temperature. They will keep for several days.

Enjoy your homemade Kokosmakronen as a sweet and coconutty treat with a cup of tea or coffee, or share them with friends and family during the holiday season!

Früchtebrot (Fruit Bread)

Ingredients:

- 1 and 1/2 cups mixed dried fruits (such as raisins, currants, chopped dates, chopped apricots, chopped figs)
- 1/2 cup chopped nuts (such as walnuts, pecans, almonds)
- 1/2 cup rum or orange juice (for soaking the dried fruits)
- 2 cups all-purpose flour
- 1 teaspoon baking powder
- 1/2 teaspoon baking soda
- 1/2 teaspoon salt
- 1 teaspoon ground cinnamon
- 1/2 teaspoon ground nutmeg
- 1/4 teaspoon ground cloves
- 1/2 cup unsalted butter, softened
- 3/4 cup packed brown sugar
- 2 large eggs
- 1 teaspoon vanilla extract
- Zest of 1 orange
- Zest of 1 lemon

Instructions:

1. In a small bowl, combine the mixed dried fruits and chopped nuts. Pour the rum or orange juice over the mixture and let it soak for at least 1 hour, or overnight, stirring occasionally.
2. Preheat your oven to 350°F (175°C). Grease and flour a 9x5-inch loaf pan or line it with parchment paper.
3. In a medium bowl, sift together the flour, baking powder, baking soda, salt, cinnamon, nutmeg, and cloves. Set aside.
4. In a large mixing bowl, cream together the softened butter and brown sugar until light and fluffy.
5. Add the eggs, one at a time, beating well after each addition. Stir in the vanilla extract, orange zest, and lemon zest.
6. Gradually add the dry ingredients to the wet ingredients, mixing until just combined.
7. Fold in the soaked dried fruits and nuts, along with any remaining liquid from the soaking process, until evenly distributed throughout the batter.

8. Pour the batter into the prepared loaf pan and smooth the top with a spatula.
9. Bake in the preheated oven for 60-70 minutes, or until a toothpick inserted into the center comes out clean and the top is golden brown.
10. Remove from the oven and let the Früchtebrot cool in the pan for 10 minutes before transferring it to a wire rack to cool completely.
11. Once cooled, slice the Fruit Bread and serve. Enjoy it plain or with a smear of butter.

Store any leftover Früchtebrot in an airtight container at room temperature for up to a week, or freeze for longer storage. Enjoy this delicious and festive treat with friends and family during the holiday season!

Buchteln (Sweet Rolls)

Ingredients:

For the dough:

- 3 and 1/2 cups all-purpose flour
- 1/4 cup granulated sugar
- 1 packet (2 and 1/4 teaspoons) active dry yeast
- 1/2 teaspoon salt
- 1 cup warm milk (about 110°F/45°C)
- 1/4 cup unsalted butter, melted
- 2 large eggs

For the filling:

- Your favorite jam or fruit compote

For the topping:

- 2 tablespoons unsalted butter, melted
- Powdered sugar for dusting

Instructions:

1. In a large mixing bowl, combine the flour, sugar, yeast, and salt for the dough.
2. Add the warm milk, melted butter, and eggs to the dry ingredients. Mix until a soft dough forms.
3. Turn the dough out onto a lightly floured surface and knead for about 5-7 minutes, or until the dough is smooth and elastic.
4. Place the dough in a greased bowl, cover with a clean kitchen towel or plastic wrap, and let it rise in a warm, draft-free place for about 1 hour, or until doubled in size.
5. Once the dough has doubled in size, punch it down to release the air bubbles. Divide the dough into equal-sized portions, depending on how large you want your Buchteln to be.

6. Take each portion of dough and flatten it into a circle. Place a spoonful of jam or fruit compote in the center of each circle.
7. Pull the edges of the dough up and over the filling, pinching the seams to seal and forming a ball shape.
8. Place the filled dough balls seam side down in a greased baking dish, leaving a little space between each one.
9. Cover the baking dish with a clean kitchen towel and let the Buchteln rise for another 30-45 minutes, or until puffy.
10. Preheat your oven to 350°F (175°C).
11. Once the Buchteln have risen, brush the tops with melted butter.
12. Bake in the preheated oven for 20-25 minutes, or until golden brown.
13. Remove from the oven and let the Buchteln cool slightly before dusting with powdered sugar.
14. Serve the Buchteln warm as a delicious dessert or sweet treat.

Enjoy your homemade Buchteln with a cup of coffee or tea for a delightful and comforting treat!

Dampfnudeln (Steamed Dumplings)

Ingredients:

For the dumplings:

- 2 and 1/4 teaspoons (1 packet) active dry yeast
- 1/4 cup warm water (about 110°F/45°C)
- 1 cup warm milk (about 110°F/45°C)
- 1/4 cup granulated sugar
- 1/4 cup unsalted butter, melted
- 1/2 teaspoon salt
- 4 cups all-purpose flour

For the cooking liquid:

- 1/2 cup water
- 1/4 cup unsalted butter
- 1/4 cup granulated sugar

Instructions:

1. In a small bowl, dissolve the active dry yeast in warm water. Let it sit for about 5 minutes, or until frothy.
2. In a large mixing bowl, combine the warm milk, sugar, melted butter, and salt. Stir until the sugar is dissolved.
3. Add the yeast mixture to the milk mixture and mix well.
4. Gradually add the flour to the wet ingredients, stirring until a soft dough forms.
5. Turn the dough out onto a lightly floured surface and knead for about 5-7 minutes, or until the dough is smooth and elastic.
6. Place the dough in a greased bowl, cover with a clean kitchen towel or plastic wrap, and let it rise in a warm, draft-free place for about 1 hour, or until doubled in size.
7. Once the dough has doubled in size, punch it down to release the air bubbles. Divide the dough into equal-sized portions, depending on how large you want your dumplings to be.

8. Shape each portion of dough into a smooth ball and place them on a greased baking sheet, leaving some space between each one.
9. In a large, deep skillet or Dutch oven, combine the water, butter, and sugar for the cooking liquid. Heat over medium heat until the butter is melted and the mixture is simmering.
10. Carefully place the dough balls into the simmering liquid, seam side down, spacing them evenly apart.
11. Cover the skillet or Dutch oven with a tight-fitting lid and reduce the heat to low. Let the dumplings steam for about 20-25 minutes, or until they have doubled in size and are cooked through.
12. Once cooked, remove the lid and let the dumplings cook for an additional 5 minutes, or until the bottoms are golden brown and crispy.
13. Remove the dumplings from the skillet or Dutch oven and serve them warm with vanilla custard sauce, fruit compote, or your favorite topping.

Enjoy your homemade Dampfnudeln as a comforting and delicious dessert or sweet treat!

Kirschplotzer (Cherry Tart)

Ingredients:

- 6 cups stale bread, cut into cubes (such as white bread or brioche)
- 1 cup milk
- 4 cups pitted cherries (fresh or frozen)
- 1/2 cup granulated sugar
- 4 large eggs
- 1/2 cup heavy cream
- 1/4 cup unsalted butter, melted
- 1 teaspoon vanilla extract
- 1/2 teaspoon ground cinnamon
- 1/4 teaspoon ground nutmeg
- Pinch of salt
- Powdered sugar, for dusting

Instructions:

1. Preheat your oven to 350°F (175°C). Grease a 9x13-inch baking dish or casserole dish.
2. In a large mixing bowl, soak the bread cubes in the milk for about 10-15 minutes, or until softened.
3. In another bowl, toss the pitted cherries with 1/4 cup of granulated sugar and set aside.
4. In a separate bowl, whisk together the eggs, heavy cream, melted butter, vanilla extract, cinnamon, nutmeg, and a pinch of salt until well combined.
5. Add the soaked bread cubes to the egg mixture and stir until evenly coated.
6. Gently fold in the prepared cherries until evenly distributed throughout the mixture.
7. Pour the mixture into the prepared baking dish, spreading it out evenly.
8. Sprinkle the remaining 1/4 cup of granulated sugar over the top of the mixture.
9. Bake in the preheated oven for 40-45 minutes, or until the top is golden brown and the pudding is set.
10. Remove from the oven and let it cool slightly before serving.
11. Dust the top with powdered sugar before serving, if desired.
12. Serve the Kirschplotzer warm as a comforting dessert, and enjoy the delicious blend of cherries, bread, and spices.

Kirschplotzer can be enjoyed on its own or with a dollop of whipped cream or a scoop of vanilla ice cream for an extra indulgent treat!

Mohntorte (Poppy Seed Tart)

Ingredients:

For the poppy seed filling:

- 1 cup poppy seeds
- 1 cup milk
- 1/2 cup granulated sugar
- 1/4 cup unsalted butter
- 2 large eggs
- 1/4 cup raisins (optional)
- Zest of 1 lemon
- 1 teaspoon vanilla extract

For the tart crust:

- 1 and 1/2 cups all-purpose flour
- 1/2 cup granulated sugar
- 1/2 cup unsalted butter, chilled and cubed
- 1 large egg
- 1 teaspoon vanilla extract
- Pinch of salt

Instructions:

1. Preheat your oven to 350°F (175°C). Grease and flour a 9-inch tart pan with a removable bottom.
2. To make the poppy seed filling, place the poppy seeds in a saucepan and cover them with milk. Bring the mixture to a simmer over medium heat, then reduce the heat to low and cook for about 10 minutes, stirring occasionally, until the poppy seeds have absorbed most of the milk. Remove from heat and let it cool slightly.
3. In a separate bowl, cream together the sugar and butter until light and fluffy. Beat in the eggs, one at a time, until well combined.
4. Stir in the cooked poppy seed mixture, raisins (if using), lemon zest, and vanilla extract until evenly distributed. Set aside.

5. To make the tart crust, in a food processor, combine the flour, sugar, chilled butter cubes, egg, vanilla extract, and salt. Pulse until the mixture resembles coarse crumbs and starts to come together.
6. Press the crust mixture evenly into the bottom and up the sides of the prepared tart pan.
7. Pour the poppy seed filling nto the tart crust and spread it out evenly.
8. Bake in the preheated oven for 35-40 minutes, or until the tart crust is golden brown and the filling is set.
9. Remove from the oven and let the Mohntorte cool completely in the tart pan before removing it.
10. Once cooled, carefully remove the Mohntorte from the tart pan and transfer it to a serving platter.
11. Slice and serve the Mohntorte at room temperature. Optionally, dust the top with powdered sugar before serving.

Enjoy your homemade Mohntorte with a cup of coffee or tea for a delightful and indulgent treat!

Linzer Torte (Linzer Tart)

Ingredients:

For the crust:

- 1 and 1/2 cups all-purpose flour
- 1/2 cup ground almonds or hazelnuts
- 1/2 cup granulated sugar
- 1/2 teaspoon ground cinnamon
- 1/4 teaspoon ground cloves
- 1/4 teaspoon salt
- 1/2 cup unsalted butter, chilled and cubed
- 1 large egg
- 1 teaspoon vanilla extract
- Zest of 1 lemon

For the filling:

- 1 cup raspberry jam or other fruit preserves
- 1/2 cup ground almonds or hazelnuts

For assembly:

- Powdered sugar, for dusting

Instructions:

1. Preheat your oven to 375°F (190°C). Grease and flour a 9-inch tart pan with a removable bottom.
2. In a food processor, combine the flour, ground almonds or hazelnuts, sugar, cinnamon, cloves, and salt. Pulse until well combined.
3. Add the chilled butter cubes to the food processor and pulse until the mixture resembles coarse crumbs.
4. In a small bowl, whisk together the egg, vanilla extract, and lemon zest. Add the egg mixture to the food processor and pulse until the dough starts to come together.
5. Turn the dough out onto a lightly floured surface and knead it gently until it forms a smooth ball.

6. Divide the dough in half. Roll out one half of the dough into a circle large enough to fit the bottom of the prepared tart pan. Carefully transfer the dough to the tart pan and press it into the bottom and up the sides.
7. Spread the raspberry jam evenly over the bottom of the crust. Sprinkle the ground almonds or hazelnuts over the jam.
8. Roll out the remaining dough into a circle and cut it into strips to create a lattice pattern on top of the tart.
9. Place the dough strips over the jam in a lattice pattern, pressing the ends into the edges of the crust to seal.
10. Trim any excess dough from the edges of the tart.
11. Bake in the preheated oven for 25-30 minutes, or until the crust is golden brown.
12. Remove from the oven and let the Linzer Torte cool completely in the tart pan.
13. Once cooled, carefully remove the Linzer Torte from the tart pan and transfer it to a serving platter.
14. Dust the top of the Linzer Torte with powdered sugar before serving.

Enjoy your homemade Linzer Torte with a cup of coffee or tea for a delicious and elegant dessert!

Schmandkuchen (Sour Cream Cake)

Ingredients:

For the cake:

- 1 and 1/2 cups all-purpose flour
- 1 teaspoon baking powder
- 1/4 teaspoon baking soda
- Pinch of salt
- 1/2 cup unsalted butter, softened
- 1 cup granulated sugar
- 2 large eggs
- 1 teaspoon vanilla extract
- 1 cup sour cream

For the topping:

- 1 cup sour cream
- 1/4 cup granulated sugar
- 1 large egg
- 1 teaspoon vanilla extract
- Pinch of salt
- Sliced almonds for garnish (optional)

Instructions:

1. Preheat your oven to 350°F (175°C). Grease and flour a 9-inch round cake pan.
2. In a medium bowl, sift together the flour, baking powder, baking soda, and salt. Set aside.
3. In a large mixing bowl, cream together the softened butter and sugar until light and fluffy.
4. Add the eggs, one at a time, beating well after each addition. Stir in the vanilla extract.
5. Gradually add the dry ingredients to the wet ingredients, alternating with the sour cream, and mix until just combined. Be careful not to overmix.
6. Pour the cake batter into the prepared cake pan and spread it out evenly.

7. In a separate bowl, whisk together the sour cream, sugar, egg, vanilla extract, and a pinch of salt until smooth.
8. Pour the sour cream topping over the cake batter in the cake pan, spreading it out evenly.
9. If desired, sprinkle sliced almonds over the top of the sour cream topping for garnish.
10. Bake in the preheated oven for 30-35 minutes, or until the cake is golden brown and a toothpick inserted into the center comes out clean.
11. Remove from the oven and let the Schmandkuchen cool in the pan for 10 minutes before transferring it to a wire rack to cool completely.
12. Once cooled, slice and serve the Schmandkuchen at room temperature.

Enjoy your homemade Schmandkuchen with its moist and tangy flavor as a delightful dessert or sweet treat!

Zwetschgenkuchen (Plum Cake)

Ingredients:

For the cake base:

- 1 and 1/2 cups all-purpose flour
- 1 teaspoon baking powder
- 1/4 teaspoon salt
- 1/2 cup unsalted butter, softened
- 3/4 cup granulated sugar
- 2 large eggs
- 1 teaspoon vanilla extract
- 1/4 cup milk

For the plum topping:

- 1 and 1/2 pounds ripe plums (Zwetschgen), halved and pitted
- 2 tablespoons granulated sugar
- 1 teaspoon ground cinnamon
- 1 tablespoon lemon juice

For the streusel topping (optional):

- 1/2 cup all-purpose flour
- 1/4 cup granulated sugar
- 1/4 cup unsalted butter, chilled and cubed

Instructions:

1. Preheat your oven to 350°F (175°C). Grease and flour a 9x13-inch baking dish or tart pan.
2. In a medium bowl, sift together the flour, baking powder, and salt. Set aside.
3. In a large mixing bowl, cream together the softened butter and sugar until light and fluffy.
4. Add the eggs, one at a time, beating well after each addition. Stir in the vanilla extract.

5. Gradually add the dry ingredients to the wet ingredients, alternating with the milk, and mix until just combined.
6. Spread the cake batter evenly into the prepared baking dish or tart pan.
7. Arrange the halved and pitted plums on top of the cake batter, cut side up, in rows or a decorative pattern.
8. In a small bowl, mix together the granulated sugar, ground cinnamon, and lemon juice. Sprinkle this mixture evenly over the plums.
9. If desired, prepare the streusel topping by combining the flour and sugar in a bowl. Cut in the chilled butter using a pastry cutter or fork until the mixture resembles coarse crumbs. Sprinkle the streusel topping over the plums.
10. Bake in the preheated oven for 40-45 minutes, or until the cake is golden brown and a toothpick inserted into the center comes out clean.
11. Remove from the oven and let the Zwetschgenkuchen cool in the pan for at least 15-20 minutes before serving.
12. Once cooled slightly, slice and serve the Plum Cake warm or at room temperature.

Enjoy your homemade Zwetschgenkuchen with its deliciously sweet and tangy plums for a delightful dessert or afternoon treat!

Birnenkuchen (Pear Cake)

Ingredients:

For the cake base:

- 1 and 1/2 cups all-purpose flour
- 1 and 1/2 teaspoons baking powder
- 1/4 teaspoon salt
- 1/2 cup unsalted butter, softened
- 3/4 cup granulated sugar
- 2 large eggs
- 1 teaspoon vanilla extract
- 1/4 cup milk

For the pear topping:

- 3-4 ripe pears, peeled, cored, and thinly sliced
- 1 tablespoon lemon juice
- 2 tablespoons granulated sugar
- 1/2 teaspoon ground cinnamon

For the streusel topping (optional):

- 1/2 cup all-purpose flour
- 1/4 cup granulated sugar
- 1/4 cup unsalted butter, chilled and cubed

Instructions:

1. Preheat your oven to 350°F (175°C). Grease and flour a 9-inch round cake pan.
2. In a medium bowl, sift together the flour, baking powder, and salt. Set aside.
3. In a large mixing bowl, cream together the softened butter and sugar until light and fluffy.
4. Add the eggs, one at a time, beating well after each addition. Stir in the vanilla extract.

5. Gradually add the dry ingredients to the wet ingredients, alternating with the milk and mix until just combined.
6. Spread the cake batter evenly into the prepared cake pan.
7. In a separate bowl, toss the thinly sliced pears with lemon juice, granulated sugar, and ground cinnamon until well coated.
8. Arrange the pear slices on top of the cake batter in a circular pattern or as desired.
9. If desired, prepare the streusel topping by combining the flour and sugar in a bowl. Cut in the chilled butter using a pastry cutter or fork until the mixture resembles coarse crumbs. Sprinkle the streusel topping over the pears.
10. Bake in the preheated oven for 40-45 minutes, or until the cake is golden brown and a toothpick inserted into the center comes out clean.
11. Remove from the oven and let the Birnenkuchen cool in the pan for at least 15-20 minutes before serving.
12. Once cooled slightly, slice and serve the Pear Cake warm or at room temperature.

Enjoy your homemade Birnenkuchen with its tender cake base and deliciously sweet pear topping for a delightful dessert or afternoon treat!

Zwetschgenknödel (Plum Dumplings)

Ingredients:

For the dough:

- 2 large potatoes, peeled and boiled until tender
- 1 and 1/2 cups all-purpose flour
- Pinch of salt
- 1 tablespoon unsalted butter, melted

For the filling:

- 12 ripe plums (Zwetschgen), pitted and halved
- 12 sugar cubes

For the breadcrumb coating:

- 1 cup breadcrumbs
- 2 tablespoons unsalted butter
- 2 tablespoons granulated sugar
- 1 teaspoon ground cinnamon (optional)

Instructions:

1. Start by preparing the dough. Mash the boiled potatoes until smooth, then let them cool slightly.
2. In a large mixing bowl, combine the mashed potatoes, flour, salt, and melted butter. Mix until a soft dough forms. If the dough is too sticky, add more flour as needed.
3. Divide the dough into 12 equal portions and shape each portion into a small ball.
4. Flatten each dough ball into a disc and place a sugar cube in the center. Wrap the dough around the sugar cube, forming a ball with the sugar cube enclosed in the center.
5. Flatten each dough ball slightly and place a halved plum, cut side down, in the center. Wrap the dough around the plum, ensuring it is completely enclosed.

6. Bring a large pot of salted water to a boil. Carefully drop the plum dumplings into the boiling water and cook for about 10-12 minutes, or until they float to the surface and are cooked through.
7. While the dumplings are cooking, prepare the breadcrumb coating. In a skillet, melt the butter over medium heat. Add the breadcrumbs and toast them until golden brown and fragrant, stirring constantly.
8. Once the breadcrumbs are toasted, add the granulated sugar and ground cinnamon (if using) to the skillet and mix well.
9. Remove the cooked dumplings from the boiling water using a slotted spoon and drain them briefly on paper towels.
10. Roll the drained dumplings in the sweetened breadcrumbs until evenly coated.
11. Serve the Zwetschgenknödel warm, sprinkled with any remaining breadcrumb mixture.

Enjoy your homemade Zwetschgenknödel as a delicious and comforting dessert, perfect for showcasing the sweet flavor of ripe plums!

Käse-Sahne-Torte (Cheese Cream Cake)

Ingredients:

For the sponge cake layers:

- 6 large eggs, at room temperature
- 3/4 cup granulated sugar
- 1 teaspoon vanilla extract
- 1 cup all-purpose flour
- 1 teaspoon baking powder
- Pinch of salt

For the cheese filling:

- 24 ounces (680g) cream cheese, softened
- 1 cup granulated sugar
- 1 teaspoon vanilla extract
- 2 cups heavy cream, chilled

For the topping:

- 1 cup fruit preserves or fresh fruit (such as strawberries, raspberries, or cherries)
- 1/4 cup water
- 1 tablespoon granulated sugar
- 1 tablespoon cornstarch

Instructions:

1. Preheat your oven to 350°F (175°C). Grease and line the bottoms of two 9-inch round cake pans with parchment paper.
2. In a large mixing bowl, beat the eggs with an electric mixer on high speed until foamy.
3. Gradually add the sugar and vanilla extract to the beaten eggs, continuing to beat until the mixture is thick and pale yellow.
4. In a separate bowl, sift together the flour, baking powder, and salt.

5. Gently fold the dry ingredients into the egg mixture until just combined, being careful not to deflate the batter.
6. Divide the batter evenly between the prepared cake pans and smooth the tops with a spatula.
7. Bake in the preheated oven for 20-25 minutes, or until the cakes are golden brown and spring back when lightly touched.
8. Remove the cakes from the oven and let them cool in the pans for 5 minutes before transferring them to wire racks to cool completely.
9. While the cakes are cooling, prepare the cheese filling. In a large mixing bowl, beat the cream cheese, sugar, and vanilla extract until smooth and creamy.
10. In a separate bowl, whip the heavy cream until stiff peaks form.
11. Gently fold the whipped cream into the cream cheese mixture until well combined. Be careful not to overmix.
12. Once the cakes are completely cooled, place one cake layer on a serving plate or cake stand.
13. Spread a generous layer of the cheese filling over the cake layer.
14. Place the second cake layer on top of the filling, pressing down gently to secure it.
15. In a small saucepan, combine the fruit preserves or fresh fruit, water, sugar, and cornstarch. Cook over medium heat, stirring constantly, until the mixture thickens and comes to a simmer.
16. Remove the fruit topping from the heat and let it cool slightly.
17. Pour the fruit topping over the top of the cake, spreading it out evenly.
18. Refrigerate the Käse-Sahne-Torte for at least 4 hours, or overnight, to allow the flavors to meld and the filling to set.
19. Before serving, slice the cake and enjoy!

This Käse-Sahne-Torte is a decadent and creamy dessert that's perfect for any special occasion or celebration. Enjoy its rich flavor and light texture with friends and family!